START TO RACE

JEFF TOGHILL / TONY HILL

DAVID & CHARLES
Newton Abbot London

Cover photograph: Greg Macbean, courtesy of *Modern Boating*.

British Library Cataloguing in Publication Data
Toghill, Jeff
Start to race.
1. Yacht racing
I. Title II. Hill, Tony
797.1'4 GV826.5
ISBN 0-7153-8413-9

First published in Australia by A.H. & A.W. Reed Pty Ltd, 1982
First published in the United Kingdom in 1983 by
David & Charles (Publishers) Ltd
Newton Abbot, Devon

Printed in Hong Kong

Contents

Introduction

There are numerous books on basic sailing. There are also numerous books which expound numerous theories on the finer points of high performance racing. But there are few — if any — which fill the gap between, guiding the average competent sailor into his first season of competitive racing.

This book fills that gap. Assuming from the outset that you have a reasonable knowledge of boat handling, it teaches you how to get into racing; how to improve your own ability and the performance of your boat; how to develop your tactical skill and make your boat go faster; how to tune yourself and your crew for competitive racing, and convert your boat from an average performer to a hot-shot racer.

Everyone likes to be a winner, and whether your racing ambitions are merely to join social weekend club racing or to 'go for the gold', this book will tell you how to go about it in the initial stages and how to come out a winner at the end.

1 Getting Geared Up

Sail-boat racing invariably means sailing clubs, which in turn means sailing people. And since sailing people, like any group of enthusiasts, talk extensively about their interest, then obviously the first thing to do in order to get started in sail-boat racing is to join a club. Sailing enthusiasts are friendly folk and you will be drawn into a discussion group picking up useful hints almost from the time you walk in the door.

Every sail-boat skipper (and to a lesser extent crew as well) is an expert in his own mind! Most experts love to expound their theories, so you will have no shortage of advice as to how to get started. Indeed, once the word gets round that you offer a sympathetic ear, you may well find the plethora of 'experts' embarrassing! But from all the friendly advice, much of which can be discarded, a steady flow of useful information will come through which will put you on the beginning of your racing path. A few judicial questions dropped into the conversation will induce information about specific aspects of the sport and form the structure from which you will determine how you intend to get started.

Don't be afraid to talk to the *real* experts — the persistent winners, the old and experienced salts and even the championship holders. Most are only too ready to give advice to a novice, and their assistance can be invaluable since they have all been through the early stages and will be aware of the pitfalls. A few hours' discussion with experts can straighten your thinking at an early stage and short-circuit some of the problems which are always faced when starting something new.

Joining a club

The first step, then, is to join a sailing club and gather as much guidance as you can from talking to other club members. You will need to join a club anyway if you intend to race, so better to join early and learn all you can, rather than wait until your boat and crew are lined up for the first starting gun. Since, as described later, preparation beforehand is a major part of the strategy in yacht racing, it is never too early to start, and joining a club even before you have bought your boat — if club rules allow — may enable you to avoid a lot of unnecessary work and expense when the practical preparation begins.

The club you join must be a recognised club affiliated with the governing body which controls racing on a national — even international — basis. Such affiliated clubs usually have an arrangement whereby you can race with any club similarly affiliated. This can widen the scope of your racing considerably, since you can choose among clubs with different venues as well as different standards and classes. If, for example, your local sailing club is the most convenient but does not race your class of boat, you can enjoy class racing with another club while still enjoying the facilities and companionship of your own local club.

Apart from learning the basic ropes from more experienced club members, there are the practical features of club life. Many clubs hold lectures or courses or seminars on the various facets of racing techniques. There are social days both on and off the water which often enable you to involve your family or friends, and quite often club membership entitles you to discounts with local chandlers or sailmakers and even, in some cases, insurance companies — an important spin-off when you are getting pennies together to fit out the boat.

Education at the club will familiarise you with details of safety requirements, racing rules and any local rules. The whole reason for joining a club prior to starting your racing career is to get to know what's going on. There is no better way to do this than to become involved with the people against whom you are going to race and learn as much from them as you can before the racing begins.

Selecting the boat

The type of boat you intend to race will be determined by a great number of factors. If you do not already own a boat, you will need to spend a great deal of time and thought before deciding which to buy. Your decision will almost invariably be a compromise, since the ultimate racing yacht may not suit you physically or financially. The financial aspect is obvious; most people have a budget and, whatever your dreams, the craft you finally purchase must fall well within that budget. Always buy well within your financial capabilities, for as one yachtsman once commented, a racing boat is just a hole in the water into which you pour money! There will always be extra pieces

Class racing is the most exciting of all forms of sail boat racing. But it has many limitations, not all of them obvious. Body weight, for example, is an important consideration with lightweight boats such as Lasers.

of gear, to say nothing of new sails and equipment, and if you stretch your budget to the limit in purchasing the boat and equipment there will be nothing left for keeping her in racing trim.

On the physical side, you will need to do a little self-analysis. Some physical aspects of racing boats are obvious — you would not buy a Laser if you weigh 95 kg, nor would you buy an ocean racer if you are extremely susceptible to seasickness! But there are other, less obvious, physical factors that must be resolved before the buying

Catamarans are exhilarating racing machines, but physically very demanding. Know your limitations when buying a racing boat.

transaction takes place. The availability of crew is one such factor. Good crewmen are not easy to come by, and unless you have a small, dedicated band who turn out for every race regardless of wind or weather, you will be in for frustration and disappointment. Having the boat tied up at the clubhouse because of an absent crewman is just as frustrating as turning in a mediocre performance in the race as a result of picking up inexperienced substitutes.

Then there is the question of your own physical capabilities. Many boats which are visually exciting can be hard to handle, and this does not apply only to large yachts. Single-handed centreboarders can be just as demanding physically. You will thus need to assess your physical ability very closely before making the final decision.

Once again, talking around the club will often bring to light factors which have considerable bearing on your purchase. Club members who have raced the boat you have in mind will offer useful advice on the basis of their experience. Having analysed their comments, you will need to sail the boat in order to form your own opinion. All

It takes only one heavy race to damage a lot of gear. Keeping the boat in action through a full racing season can be an expensive exercise.

boats are different and require different handling; to assume that you can handle a flighty centreboarder because you are experienced with medium-class keel boats is to invite possible disaster.

Avoiding all these pitfalls and purchasing the ideal boat for your racing plans will only come as a result of a lot of talking, a lot of researching and a lot of foot-slogging!

The racing gear

No matter what its basic hull design, the fittings on a boat used for racing are a far cry from those on a boat used solely for cruising. Comfort is the keynote in cruising craft, and other than the basic sailing gear the major items involved in fitting out will be galley stoves, settee cushions and the like. By contrast, these luxuries will rarely appear aboard a true racing yacht for they create unnecessary weight. In this type of craft the emphasis is on 'go-fast' gear, ranging from a large wardrobe of sails down to simple items such as tweakers.

Obviously the racing gear fitted to a basic boat will vary considerably according to class and size. Centreboarders often need little more than a few fancy gadgets to obtain maximum performance. Indeed, some are so designed that strict conformation to class rules and measurements eliminates the need to fit any extra gear at all. By contrast, a high-performance, ocean-racing yacht may be draped with gear until it looks like a sea-going Christmas tree.

It follows, then, that a detailed guide to fitting out all types and sizes of racing craft would be quite impossible, so for the purposes of this book we shall assume we have a boat with basic cruising rig and add the necessary basic gear to improve her performance to racing standard.

Most boats set up for cruising do not allow for sufficient adjustments to the rig and sails when racing. The equipment described here will allow the racing helmsman not only to adjust the tension on various parts of the gear in order to obtain maximum performance in all weather conditions, but also to obtain an indication of wind direction and the flow of air over the sails. This will enable him to steer an accurate course and also determine what adjustments must be made for the boat to go faster.

In order to offer a base level from which to determine the requirements of each individual craft, we shall assume that we have the basic hull and rig of an average, small-keel boat. To convert this boat for racing, the following gear is essential:

1 Wind indicators

A masthead wind indicator is considered a must by all experienced racing helmsmen. The mast cap is the only part of the boat where the wind is relatively undisturbed and both visual and electronic wind indicators are mounted here. It is essential for all prospective racing helmsmen first to learn to sail their boat by eye and by the feel of the helm. Electronic instruments may well improve your performance at a later date when you have gained the necessary basic experience. Until then, you should concentrate on the visual approach, watching the sails and tufts and using the masthead wind indicator. The type with fixed arms is the best, particularly when sailing downwind, as the apparent wind is hard to observe. The fixed arms give points of reference against which to determine the wind direction, bearing in mind that you are looking at the sky and thus relative wind direction may be hard to spot.

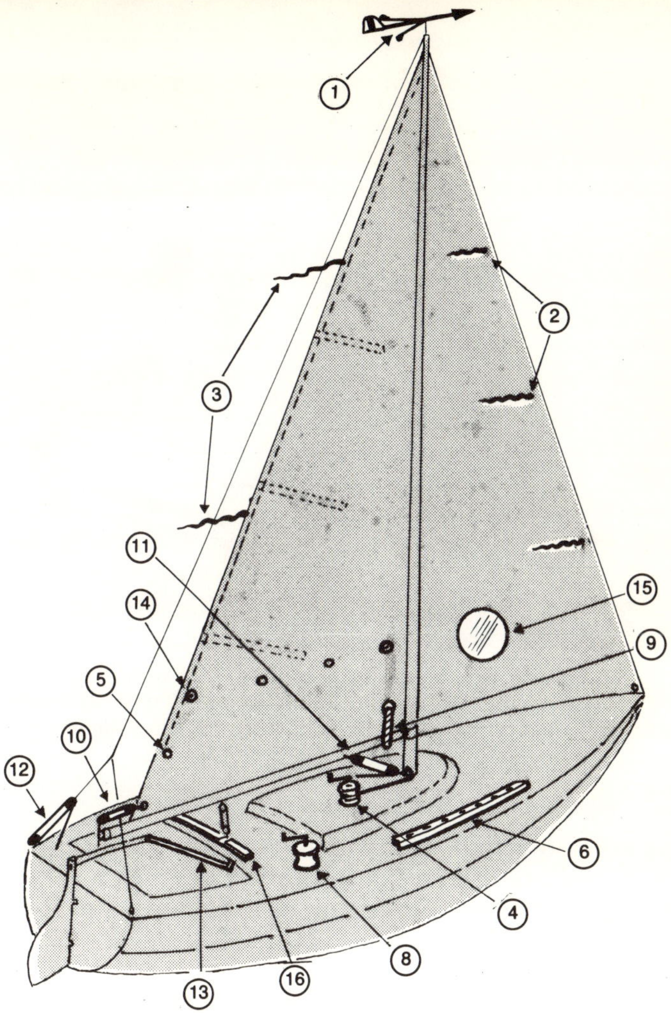

Principal go-fast gear required for improving a yacht's racing performance. Numbers relate to the description of each item in the text.

2 Steering tufts

These are usually placed near the luff of the headsail and are of great assistance in setting the sails. Providing the tufts are correctly located and the sail is not stretched, the maximum drive will be gained when the tufts on both sides of the sail are streaming horizontally, indicating a good airflow over the sail. Some keen racing yachtsmen have tufts elsewhere on the headsail and also on the mainsail to facilitate sail trimming and ensuring that all parts of both sails are gaining maximum performance.

Tufts in the headsail give an excellent indication of wind flow over the sail. In this picture they are just beginning to 'break' and the boat's performance could be improved by falling off the wind slightly.

3 Leech ribbons

These are stitched at various points to the leech of the mainsail and are used as an indication of leech and foot tension as well as correct setting of the mainsail to the wind.

4 Halyard adjustment

Instead of just pulling up the headsail and cleating it, the halyard should be led to a winch so that the luff tension may be altered while sailing. This allows adjustment of the angle of attack of the leading edge to the wind, and also moves the position of the drive in the sail. Greater tension in the halyard moves the drive further forward in the sail, and vice versa. A good system is to mark the halyard so that correct tensions can be duplicated.

5 Leech line

Nothing is more irritating than a vibration in the last few centimetres of a sail. While this may sometimes be indicative of an adjustment required to the shape of the sail, often a gentle pressure on the leech line can remove the flutter. Severe fluttering, which cannot be removed by the use of the leech line, will require the sail to be reshaped by the sailmaker.

6 Headsail sheeting tracks

These should be located on the deck in such a position as to allow maximum adjustment of sheeting positions for any headsail. They should be of a type that enable the sheeting blocks to be moved easily, to obtain the best sheeting angle of varying headsails in all weather conditions.

7 Barber-haulers (shown below)

On the more sophisticated racing boats, a small block-and-tackle arrangement is often used which allows the headsail sheeting angle to be moved both up and down as well as in and out. This gear is a refinement of the

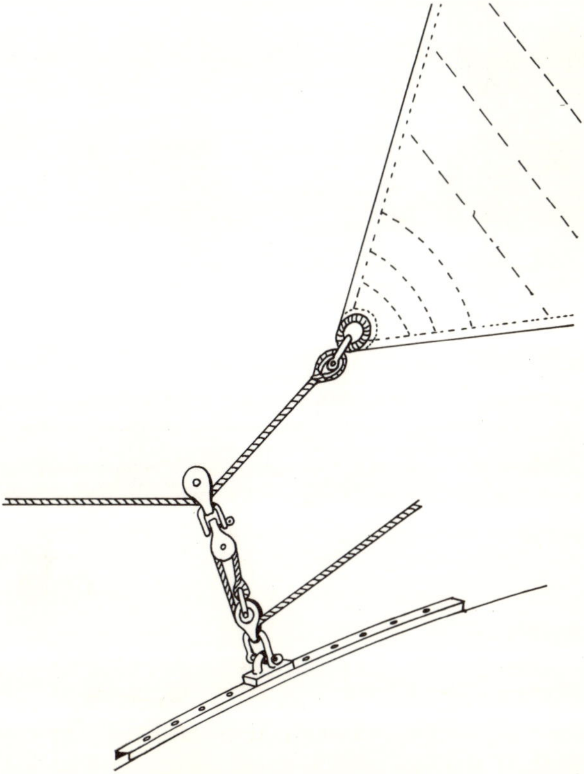

Basic form of barber-hauler.

sheeting tracks, giving more flexibility and, though not entirely essential, can provide useful fine adjustment of the headsail for high performance racing.

8 Sheet winches

It is essential that sheet winches are of sufficient power for the sails they serve and are equipped with a removable handle at the top. Fixed handles are a nuisance in fast tacking since the sheet tends to become fouled around the handle. The angle at which the winch is mounted on the coaming is also important, as riding turns can again cause fouling when making fast tacks. Geared winches allow for fast, easy adjustment even when the sail is under considerable pressure.

Correct location of sheet winches to allow easy running of the sheets with no riding turns is essential for fast, unhindered manoeuvring.

9 Cunningham Eye

This equipment, made popular by Briggs Cunningham, the famous American twelve-metre sailor, is used to tension the luff of the mainsail. It consists of a cringle set into the luff of the sail with a small, downhaul tackle secured through it. Adjustment to the luff tension is made by taking up or easing back the tackle, drawing the eye down towards the boom or vice versa. It allows for fine adjustment of the tension in the luff more quickly and more accurately than using the halyard or downhaul.

10 Clew outhaul

Simply tying off the clew of the mainsail to the end of the boom does not allow for any foot adjustment. Most boats have some form of tension gear which is essential if the boat is used for racing. Indeed, adjustment of the foot tension is as important as luff tension if the maximum performance is to be obtained from the mainsail.

11 Boom vang (kicking strap)

This tackle holds the boom down against its tendency to rise when the sheet is eased, keeping the mainsail efficient and constant in performance. The vang should be adjustable, so that sail shape can be changed according to conditions; too much tension can spoil the shape of a sail just as easily as too little tension. Easing the vang allows the end of the boom to rise, thus releasing pressure and reducing weather helm as well as the tendency to broach.

12 Backstay tensioner

The backstay is frequently adjusted to counter changing conditions. There are many different types of equipment which achieve this, ranging from a small tackle at the foot of the backstay bridle to hydraulic tensioning gear. The main purpose of backstay tension is to take up forestay sag which in turn means sag in the jib luff. In so doing the mast is bent, particularly in non-masthead rigs. The effect of mast bend varies considerably, but principally involves moving the drive in the mainsail to obtain the best shape in the sail under all weather conditions.

13 Tiller extension

This should be attached to the end of the tiller by a universal joint. The principal advantage of the extension is to allow the helmsman to position himself where he is comfortable and where his weight is most beneficial to the boat's performance. In addition, of course, he must be able to obtain good visibility all around the boat both as a safety factor and to watch the tactical movements of other boats

Without a long tiller extension the skipper could not add his weight to the team out on the trapezes.

in the race. A tiller extension is most useful in smaller yachts and absolutely essential in catamarans and centreboarders.

14 Reefing gear

There are three principal types of reefing gear — roller reefing, slab reefing and jiffy reefing. Roller reefing is not used generally for racing craft since it tends to destroy the shape of the sail and in addition causes the boom to droop into the cockpit. Slab and jiffy reefing are almost identical in effect, using reefing cringles sewn into the sail. The principal difference is that jiffy reefing is much faster and simpler than slab reefing.

Reefing reduces the sail area of the mainsail in heavy weather, without destroying the sail shape. The procedure is to engage a new tack and clew which are positioned higher up the sail, drawing them down to the boom by means of a tackle while at the same time easing away the

A mainsail designed to carry three reefs. Reinforcing at the luff and leech indicate the location of new tack and clew cringles respectively while reefing points across the sail indicate the location of the new foot. Reefing lines are already secured to the two lower clew cringles in preparation for fast reefing. The arrow on the sail is the sailmaker's badge and is not related to the reefing gear.

main halyard. Slab reefing is effected by simply tying off the new clew and tack as well as other cringles across the sail, using small reefing lines at each point. Jiffy reefing utilises a tackle secured to the new clew to draw down the leech, while at the same time the halyard eases the new tack down to a fastening on the gooseneck. Because of its speed of operation, jiffy reefing is more favoured on racing boats than the other systems.

15 Sail windows

Windows allow better vision through the headsails when sailing in close quarters. Because they create a weakness in the sail, they are not usually fitted to large offshore racing craft but are important for small, fast-performance boats sailing in congested racing conditions.

16 Mainsheet traveller
The location of the mainsheet can change the shape of the mainsail, so adjustment is made by using a sliding block on a traveller. In light weather the traveller is brought to the centre of the boat or even slightly to windward when close-hauled, to avoid back-winding of the mainsail by big headsails. In heavy weather the leech of the main is straightened and pressure relieved by setting the traveller down to leeward. Lanyards or trackstops must be fitted to hold the mainsheet in position at the required point along the traveller.

Spinnaker gear

The spinnaker is essentially a racing sail, and obtaining maximum performance with the spinnaker can increase the boat's speed quite considerably. Assuming that the boat is already fitted with basic spinnaker gear, the following refinements are often added to improve racing performance:

1 *Pole lift* This is in effect a halyard or topping lift fitted to the top of the spinnaker pole and reeved through a

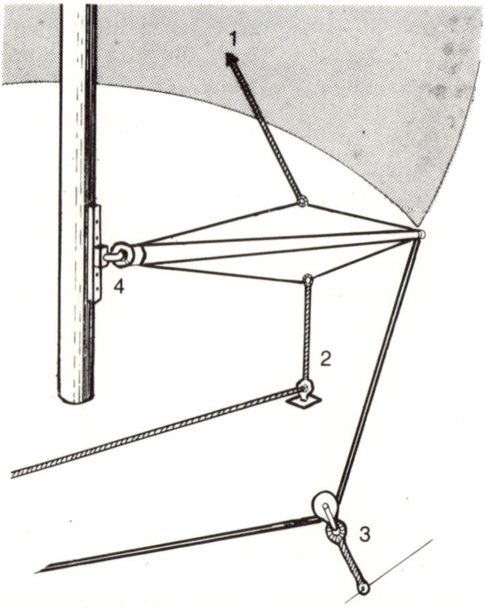

Diagram illustrating basic go-fast spinnaker gear. Numbers relate to descriptions in text.

sheave some distance up the mast. It is used to control the angle of the spinnaker pole in the vertical plane in conjunction with the pole downhaul.

2 *Pole downhaul* This consists of a bridle on the underside of the pole to which is attached a downhaul line rove through a sheave on the deck. The raising and lowering of the boom is achieved by hauling on the lift and easing the downhaul or vice versa.

3 *Tweakers* These are basically similar to barber-haulers and consist of a line secured to the boat carrying a light block which runs free along the spinnaker sheet and brace. Tweakers are used mostly to tension the brace and sheet in heavy weather to reduce oscillation at the head of the spinnaker. They are also used for retrieving the sheet when dropping the sail.

4 *Sliding spinnaker ring* This is a normal spinnaker ring fitted to a slide which travels vertically up and down the front of the mast on a track and is controlled by a system of lanyards somewhat similar to that used on the mainsheet traveller. The movement of the ring along this track enables the pole to be raised and lowered and the shape of the sail to be altered according to the weight and angle of the breeze.

5 *Turtle or spinnaker bag* This is merely a receptacle for the spinnaker so that it can be kept under control while preparing the spinnaker gear. A popular type of turtle is a

Two useful additions to normal spinnaker gear: a 'turtle' holds the bent-on spinnaker preventing it from blowing all over the place; and side netting prevents sheets and headsail (when lowered) from falling overside.

A clear illustration of a jockey pole and its main purpose of creating a better sheeting angle for the brace (guy).

specially constructed bag with a metal hoop holding the mouth open and a loosely fitted lid. An equally popular one is the ordinary plastic wash basket which is lightly lashed in the eyes of the bow, to the pulpit if fitted. All corners of the spinnaker are laid out from the mouth of the turtle so that they can be quickly snapped on to sheet, halyard and brace. This way the sail can be totally rigged while being contained within the turtle thus avoiding the possibility of it blowing around before hoisting.

6 *Jockey pole* This is a small pole fitted athwartships between the mast and the brace (guy) on larger boats when running on a close reach. It has a twofold purpose of increasing the angle between the brace and the spinnaker pole and also preventing the brace from chafing on the shrouds.

2 Pre-race Preparation

The 'cockpit check'

Having fitted the boat out with the extra racing gear, the next step is to prepare her for the first race. A good example to follow here is the routine an aircraft pilot follows prior to take off. Conscious of the fact that if something comes adrift while he is flying he may not be able to remedy or repair it, he makes a thorough check of all his instruments and gear, testing each part to ensure that it is in perfect working order.

In just the same way, you check every part of the boat's equipment and gear before the start of the race. Even a simple shackle pin coming loose can cause major problems once the race has started. At best you will lose time trying to fix it; at worst you may have to pull out of the race and return to the clubhouse. Winning a race is hard enough with every bit of gear in place and working efficiently. With loose or inefficient gear you will have no chance. Imagine the chagrin of working your way up to the lead, only to sacrifice the race because of a lost shackle pin!

So the analogy of the pilot with his check-list is a good one. Long before the race is due to begin, make a systematic check of all the boat's gear. Make sure that it is all on board and working correctly. Even champions have arrived ready to start, only to discover they have left behind an important piece of equipment (such as a sail). A systematic 'cockpit check' will avoid this type of thing happening and ensure that when you cross the starting line, you will be confident in the knowledge that your boat and gear are in tip-top shape.

Standing rigging

Start with the shackle pins. Nothing is more likely to cause a failure of rigging than a loose shackle pin. In the old days of galvanized shackles with an eye in the pin, the best system was to wire the pin in place. Stainless steel shackles tend not to have an eye, so probably the best type to use is the screw pin which is fastened in place with a screwdriver.

Apart from being driven home firmly with the screwdriver, these pins fit flush into their shackles, leaving nothing protruding to snag on a loose rope.

Similarly, check all locking nuts on turnbuckles to ensure that they are firmed down, for the flopping action of leeward shrouds can cause turnbuckles to slacken, thus setting the mast out of tune, or come undone altogether, bringing down the mast.

While on the subject of standing rigging, check the wire just above each swage as this is the most likely place for deterioration to start. The wire in the swage is held rigid, while the standing part is alternatively stressed and slackened as the boat goes from one tack to another. This causes fatigue in the metal at the point where the rigging enters the swage. The most widely used rigging wire — 1 x 19 stainless steel — is often subject to this problem.

Much the same applies at the tangs, which should swing freely to avoid the likelihood of fatigue at the upper swage.

A quick check of the rigging will indicate any sign of deterioration by stranding or whiskering. The most common areas for this to begin are in the vicinity of the spreader and also at the bridle on the backstay where the rigging wire may be bent through a fairly severe angle.

Running rigging

One of the most aggravating ways of losing a race is to have a halyard jam at the masthead, and the most common cause of this is the halyard jumping off the sheave. Check that all halyards are running freely over their sheaves and the sheaves themselves are running smoothly and evenly with no wear at the pin. At the same time check the halyards for any whiskering and deterioration, for a halyard carrying away in the middle of the race almost certainly means the end of the race for that boat.

Check all working parts of the running gear, particularly swivels and clips, for valuable time can be lost trying to open a 'frozen' spinnaker clip in the frantic moments at the start of a downwind leg. Check freedom of movement of outhauls and downhauls and the various items of adjustment such as sliding tracks, winches and cleats. A cleat that will not release freely and quickly can lose minutes at a vital point in the race!

It is important to ensure that the standing rigging is correctly tuned if the boat is to give her best performance. Equally important is to ensure that, once tuned, nothing can work loose or come undone during the race.

Sails

A quick check of the stitching will often indicate any possibility of the sail blowing out in a squall, so it is well worth making this check well ahead of time and rushing the sail to the sailmaker for restitching. Batten pockets are notorious for this, as are leaches in way of their control lines. Check that the battens are set into their pockets correctly, for, in light weather particularly, an inverted batten can cause loss of power in the sail.

Sails get an awful flogging in the course of any race but never more so than in a spill. Stitching and batten pockets are the first to go and must be checked thoroughly before each race.

The hull

No amount of 'go-fast' gear will win a race if the hull is not clean. Before each race pull the boat into shallow water and clean off her bottom. Most anti-fouling paint allows the use of a scrubbing brush without too much deterioration.

While cleaning off the underwater area, check the rudder pintles to see that they are not becoming slack, and at the same time check out any underwater equipment such as the log impeller.

The test sail

You should allow yourself at least an hour to check the boat out under sail before moving to the starting area. Having checked the equipment in the static condition, it is equally important to see that everything is working under stress. Check that the sails are set correctly for the weather conditions — in particular, that the sheeting points are in the right position, and the Cunningham Eye and other tension adjusting gear is correctly set. The mast should stand as straight as possible athwartships when under load. Check the set of the standing rigging to see that this is achieved and at the same time, check the turn and balance of the boat on all points of sailing.

A mast that is tuned to stand straight athwartships gives the best performance on any tack.

If you give yourself time for this test sail, there will always be time for adjustment if something is out of balance or requires further adjustment. Set the spinnaker and check it; at the same time give your crew the feel of the sail and the gear under less hectic conditions than those that will be experienced once the race starts.

Check your timepiece and instruments, if fitted. A sheet hand (usually the navigator) should be designated to handle the stopwatch to enable the skipper to concentrate on the start. Make sure that, as skipper, you are familiar with the flags that will be used and any other race instruction issued by the Race Committee, the course you are to follow, and any factors such as tidal streams which will need to be taken into consideration during the race. Larger boats equipped with VHF radio will be able to stay informed of any likely changes in the course, or postponements of the start, if the Committee Boat(s) is talking on the air. But keep an eye peeled for the actual signal flags, both at the start and on the Committee Boats which may be at the marks. Many races are lost because skippers don't notice last minute changes of instructions; the course can be shortened, for example, even after a race has begun.

Get an early start

The test sail is almost as important as the race itself; scrambling aboard the boat a few minutes before the start leaves no time for adjustments and repairs. The skipper who gets his crew out a couple of hours earlier and puts the boat through a thorough test sail is the skipper who is most likely to go into the race with the advantage of a trouble-free boat and a well-prepared crew.

Checking and tuning, and checking again is the only way to ensure that your boat is ready.

One of the most common mistakes in club racing is the belief among skippers and crew that a boat which performed well in the previous race will be ready for the next. But the gear may be stretched or worn, pins may have worked loose, and in any case weather conditions may require different sails. Time spent before the start of each race testing and checking the boat and her gear, and adjusting to the existing conditions is time well spent, and will ensure that both the boat and the crew are worked up

Getting down to the club early means plenty of time to check all the gear and even carry out minor repairs if needs be. Apart from a 'static' check-out, the boat must also be thoroughly checked while under sail prior to the start.

A test run before the start sorts out the crew as well as the boat, settles keyed-up nerves and gets everyone slotted into their routine.

to a high pitch when the boat crosses the starting line.

Nothing is more certain to cause disaster than panic; and nothing is more likely to cause panic on board than to have something go wrong in the heat of the race. Checking out the boat with a thorough test routine not only ensures that everything works and is unlikely to carry away, but also settles the crew into their routine. Then, if a mishap does occur, each crew man knows his job and moves smoothly and efficiently to rectify the problem. A sudden clamour of all hands to adjust something that gets out of place will cause more harm than good. Each crew man must have a set job, must know it, and be settled into it by the time the boat commences the race.

Likewise the skipper

Probably there is little need to say more than that — likewise the skipper! The tension on a skipper begins to build up as the start of the race approaches. Yet nothing is worse than to be keyed up to fever pitch when the starter's gun goes off. Nervous tension means nervous reactions, which are invariably clumsy. Both skipper and crew must be totally relaxed and confident when the starter's gun goes off, for relaxation is the key to smooth, efficient reflexes and these motivate smooth efficient operations.

A nervous, jumpy skipper will confuse both his crew and himself. There must only be one person giving orders which should be given quietly and firmly without hesitation. Quiet, calm orders convey to the crew a sense of well-being and confidence and induce a similar reaction. The best from the skipper will get the best from his crew. A thorough test sail again is essential to slacken the nervous tension and steady the butterflies. The skipper and crew, as well as the boat and gear, will be tuned to peak efficiency. As the boat lines up for the start, each man is quietly confident of his own ability and the ability of the boat to win the race.

3 The Start

Which end of the line?

The prime object of every yacht crossing the starting line is to get to the first mark before anyone else. Obviously if one end of the starting line is closer to the mark than the other, then the boats starting at that end will have an advantage. This is particularly the case when the start is to windward. One end of the line is often farther upwind than the other and thus closer to the windward mark. (This is known as a biased line.) Your first tactic should be to determine which end of the line this is, and plan your starting manoeuvres around it.

There are various ways of determining which is the windward end of the line; the following are three generally accepted methods:

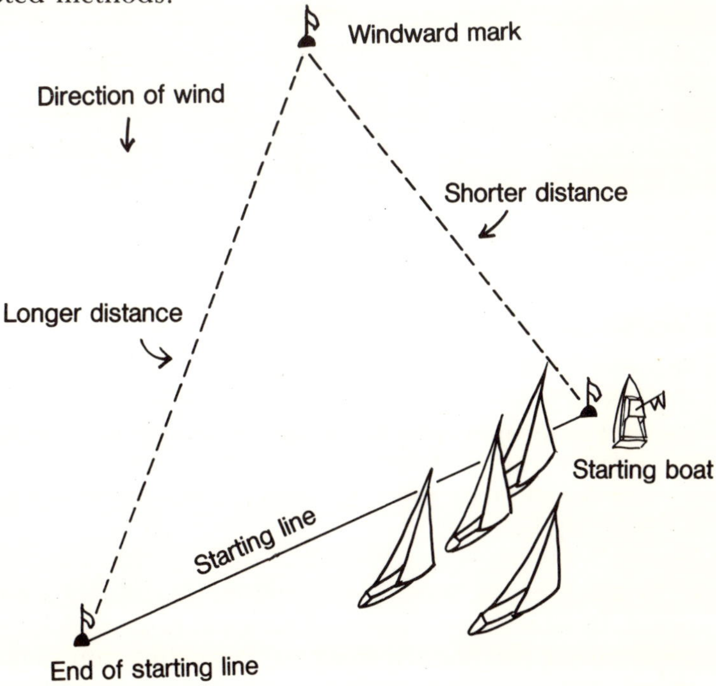

Windward starting lines are usually biased and therefore one leg to the windward mark is shorter than the other.

1 Sail directly along the line in both directions with identical sheet trim. The sails will tend to luff and collapse more with the boat heading in one direction than in the other, that direction being towards the windward end of the line.

2 Somewhere around the centre of the line, throw the boat up into the wind and hold her directly head to wind. Sight along the beam bearing (the traveller or any thwartship line will do) on either side. The windward end of the line will be the one forward of the beam bearing.

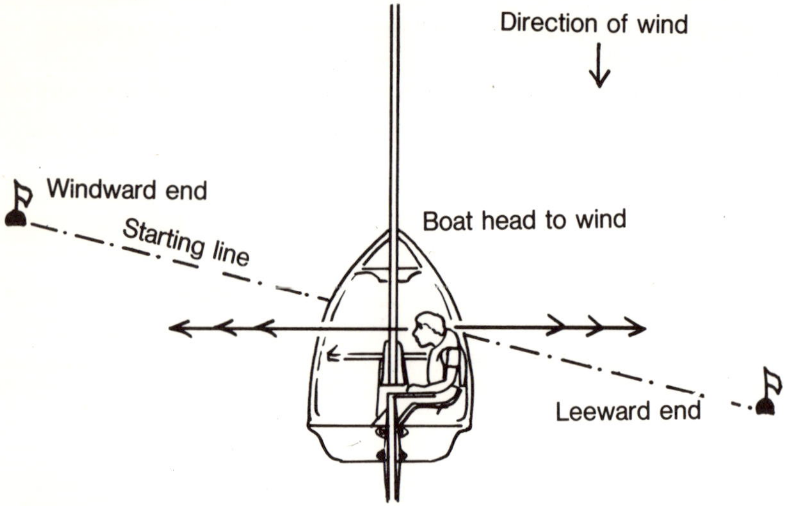

By sighting along the beam bearing of the boat when she is head to wind, the windward and leeward ends of the starting line become obvious.

3 If you have a compass aboard, head the boat to wind and determine which end of the line gives a smaller relative angle. Or else go on to first port and then starboard tacks and relate the compass bearings to the starting line.

Sometimes the starting line will be set directly across wind, in which case there will be an even start at every point along the line. In this case, providing you make a good start, your best tactic is to start at the right hand end of the line on a starboard tack which immediately puts you in a most favourable position. However, shrewd race

When everything else is equal, starboard tack is the most advantageous on which to make a windward start.

officials tend to counteract such manoeuvres and level the advantages by angling the line slightly to windward at the left end. Hence the importance of determining which end of the line lies to windward. Despite this, however, the starboard tack is still usually the most advantageous on which to cross the starting line.

Timing the start

It goes without saying that an important factor in a good start is to cross the line as close to the firing of the gun as possible. But equally important is the fact that you cross the line at full speed. Stalling around in the vicinity of the line with the boat almost stationary in the water and then pulling on the sheets as the gun goes off is a pointless exercise. Within seconds you will be swamped by other boats moving fast from behind, overtaking you and leaving you wallowing in their water and wind wash! A sailboat takes time to get under way, and if the best possible start is to be made she must not only cross the line close to the gun, but cross it at maximum available speed.

With this in mind, the pre-race manoeuvring should be made with the object of hitting the line in the required position at the required time and at full speed. Having determined which end of the line you will start and communicated this to your crew, you then make a series of

Timing the start correctly and crossing the line at full speed has put the two boats at left in a very advantageous position over the rest of the fleet

runs at the line to determine the boat's speed. The speed can, of course, be controlled by easing the sheets to slow the boat or pulling away to improve speed.

At the one-minute gun you should, ideally, be in a position slightly to windward of the track you have planned for your starting run and under such control that the boat, moving at full speed should either hit the line or be within half a boat's length of it when the gun goes off. Failing this you will lose the start, for the boats ahead will take your wind, putting you in a disadvantaged position from which it will be difficult to extricate yourself. The object of being to windward of the track is to allow

Making the run for the line. Previous trial runs should have the boat and crew tuned to the point where you cross the line at full speed right on the gun and in clear wind. Other boats, of course, have exactly the same plans!

freedom to fall away and pick up speed when the decisive moment arrives.

Problems at the start

If there are no other boats around, following the procedure described above is relatively easy. In practice, however, with possibly dozens of other boats having the same thing in mind, there will be all kinds of problems. The most common of these are likely to be:

1 *Barging* This is the term given to attempts by windward boats to push you down to leeward, particularly on a

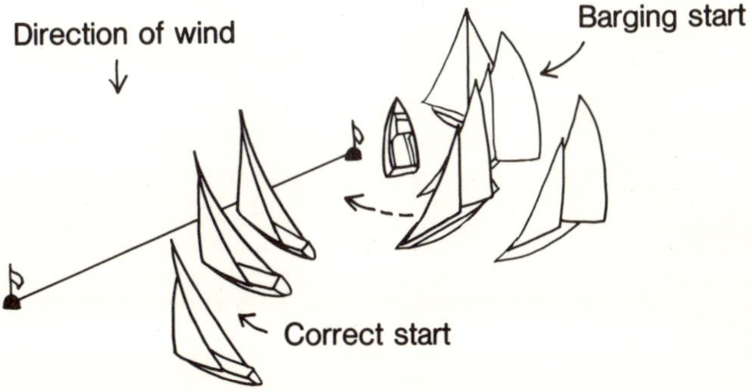

Illustrating a 'barging' start.

A classic 'barging' position. Boat 113 has the right of way and has made a good start, providing he is not intimidated by the two windward craft.

Boat 113 allowed himself to be barged out and has lost his advantage, falling away to leeward and being covered by the wind shadow of the two windward craft.

biased line. It is easily cured since you have the right of way and you must force the other boats up to windward not only to prevent them interfering with your starting run but also to keep your leeward area clear to allow room for falling off and picking up speed when required. Remember, however, that you may only luff before the gun goes off and not afterwards, unless you have cleared the line.

2 *Leeward boats forcing you up to windward* This is the reverse of the previous problem and in this case you cannot rely on right-of-way, since you are the windward boat. The answer is to be ahead of these leeward craft so that they cannot push you up.

3 *A wall of boats ahead barely moving as they wait for the gun* This is a common problem, particularly if you have chosen a point on the starting line also selected by a number of other skippers. There are two possible answers to this, the first — mentioned earlier — that the boat moving at full speed when the gun goes off will sweep past those that are hovering. If you see a spot through the wall your initial impetus could carry you through while the other boats are frantically sheeting on to get under way. If the wall is impregnable, then the second procedure is to pull away until a clear spot does appear, for the advantage of increased speed through pulling away, plus avoiding the risk of having your wind blocked, will give you a better start even though it might be slightly downwind of your original intention.

What it all boils down to, then, is that a good start revolves around two basic principles — keeping the boat moving so that at the moment the gun goes off she is at full speed and close to the line, and staying in clear air even if it means giving away your preferred starting position on the line. This means that your crew must be as much on their toes as you are, since the sheets must be trimmed to their optimum before the gun goes off.

If the boat is not moving water will not flow over the rudder and she will not be under control. So both from a point of view of speed as well as control, it is vitally important to have her moving fast before the gun goes off.

Judging your run

Judging your distance from the line requires a lot of experience. Somehow, as you begin that last dash, it always seems much farther than you estimated. It is obviously vitally important to be able to judge the position of the line if you are going to make a good start, for quite apart from the possibility of getting other boats in ahead of you, destroying your clear air, you can also be in trouble if you are ahead of time and cross the line before the gun goes off. It follows that you should be out there making dummy runs at the line as much as possible before the start to ensure that neither of these mishaps occurs.

One of the best ways of assessing your position in relation to the line is to obtain a transit prior to the start. By lining up either mark with a shore object when on the line you will be able to determine as you make your run just how far you have to go. A foreward hand should be designated to watch this transit and call its position from the bow. Similarly, someone should be timing the start on a stopwatch and calling the seconds as the gun time

Judging the run to the line put the two leading boats in an advantageous position ahead of the rest of the fleet. Such an advantage is very important in high performance boats.

approaches. You, as skipper, will have your hands full manoeuvring the boat for the start and have no time to be looking at stopwatches or transits.

The downwind start

The basic procedures for a downwind start are much the same as those to windward. The end of the line closest to the mark is the obvious one to aim for, although if the start is dead downwind often it is better to try to cross the line at an angle and thus go off on a broad reach rather than running dead square which is usually slower. Making practice runs at the line in order to judge your speed is as important as when starting to windward, although bear in mind that you will probably break out a spinnaker before reaching the line, a factor which must be taken into consideration when judging your starting run. The spinnaker should be stopped up and only broken out when you are sure of your timing, for breaking the line on a downwind run with the spinnaker flying means a time-consuming restart and one which will put you well back in the race.

The leading boats have their spinnakers set and drawing while less experienced craft are just crossing the start line with sails still not hoisted. The spinnaker start calls for crucial timing as a recall for a false start means dropping the big sail and starting again.

4 The Windward Leg

It is on the windward leg that most of the tactical manoeuvring takes place. So that you, as skipper, can concentrate on such tactics it is essential that the crew do their job without waiting for orders. Although you will always need to keep an eye aloft to see that the sails are properly trimmed, there should be no other distractions and you should be able to apply your whole concentration to keeping the boat moving fast and manoeuvring as tactics dictate.

Making the boat go fast

There are many factors involved in making the boat go fast to windward. Since this is the leg where more races are won and lost, it is well worth taking time out at this point to examine in detail these go-fast factors. Together with pointing ability, speed through the water produces good or bad windward performance which in turn usually means good or bad over-all racing performance.

Unfortunately there is no single simple method of making a boat point and foot well. Like all other aspects of sailboat racing, it is a combination of many factors involving hull, sails and crew that produce the required performance. The difference in the weight of wind is also a vitally important factor, for techniques used in light winds may be totally different — even opposite — to those used in a heavy weight of breeze. For this reason, the go-fast factors described here are segmented according to the strength of the wind and the techniques described are the best for that weight of wind.

These factors are not necessarily the most important, nor are they in any specific order. But they do form the basis of good techniques to which refinements may be added as you gain racing experience and skill.

Placement of crew

The question of whether the skipper should sit to windward or leeward is one that provokes many an

A perfectly balanced boat and crew. Cockpit crew are alert and well located, jib sheet hand keeping a lookout to leeward. The forward hand would be better lying on the foredeck where he would create less windage.

The placement of crew is correct, with the weight to the windward side, but there is insufficient crew in the cockpit and no-one to leeward to keep a lookout. Also the girls are concentrating more on the camera than their job!

argument in the club bar. While there are advantages in both, the windward position would seem to be preferable. From this position you can watch approaching weather — such as 'cat's paws' or surface turbulence — as it moves in from windward, whereas from the leeward helm position this is not possible. Then again, every sailboat has slight weather helm and apart from the fact that a pulling action on the tiller is more natural than a pushing action, if a sudden knock-down swings the boat temporarily out of control, recovery will be much simpler from the windward position than pushing uphill from below.

Visibility all round is possible from the high (windward) side, an important factor where tight manoeuvring is involved. From the leeward position the skipper must rely to a great extent on his lookouts on the high side to tell him what is approaching. Also, the tufts in the main are better seen when you are seated to windward.

The placement of the crew is different for each individual boat, depending on size and trim. An important factor, however, is keeping a lookout. All crew should act as lookouts, since other craft can appear from all

Location of crew is much more important in small craft where the trim of the boat can be considerably affected by even small movements of weight. A boat will only perform at her best when she sails on her designed waterline.

directions. Apart from the risk of collision, it is important that the skipper is notified of any tactical moves made by other craft in the race for you cannot have eyes everywhere and another boat can spring a quick tactical surprise while you are preoccupied with a manoeuvre or with the action of someone else in a different direction.

Crew weight

Since the trim of the boat is important to her performance, the placement of crew weight can have an important bearing on the boat's speed in all but large keel yachts. This is particularly the case in very light winds, where the trim of the boat is controlled almost entirely by the distribution of weight on board. It is also important, however, in stronger winds where the weight of the crew can be used to counteract excessive heel thus avoiding the need to spill wind from the sails.

A sailboat always turns in her best performance at her optimum angle of heel. This is the point at which the boat

On small centreboarders the skipper's weight is the sole trimming and balancing factor, hence body weight is important when sailing such craft in performance racing.

gains the maximum pressure in the sails without heeling to the point where the lateral resistance of the keel is diminished. The optimum angle of heel obviously varies from boat to boat but in all cases it is as close to the upright as is possible. In theory, a boat gives her best sailing performance when she is completely upright but this, of course, is not feasible. But the aim is nevertheless to sail the boat as upright as you can while gaining the maximum available drive from the wind.

Here, then, is the need to use crew weight, particularly in small craft, as a righting lever to counteract the heel. In differing wind conditions crew weight should be distributed as follows:

Light airs Trim the boat so that she is slightly heeled to leeward, particularly if there is insufficient wind to fill the sails. This means putting the crew down to leeward, the contrary position to most other wind conditions. The reason is that a boat sitting absolutely vertical in the water, or wallowing in a windless chop, causes the sails to flop down in a shapeless mess, and any light airs that may be around will not be gathered up to produce drive. By heeling the boat slightly out of the vertical, the weight of the sail cloth tends to form the sail into its correct aerofoil shape so that when a whisper of wind comes along the maximum benefit is derived from it. Fore and aft trim should generally be level with the water line except in very light airs, when a slight bow-down attitude tends to reduce the wetted area and thus the drag of the hull too.

Medium breezes In these conditions, the heel of the boat will be to leeward and the crew weight is utilized to counteract the heel and keep her as close to upright as possible. Fore and aft trim, as before, is level with the water line.

Heavy winds Now the crew need to be swung out to windward as far as possible, sitting out on the windward deck of keelboats as the rules permit, or if in dinghies, using the appropriate trapezes or similar counter-balancing gear to keep the boat as near to her optimum heel as possible without spilling wind from the mainsail. In this situation, don't forget to ensure that at least one member

Body weight right out to windward and boat trimmed level — classic heavy breeze position. Not forgetting, of course, to keep a lookout to leeward.

of the crew is keeping a good lookout from leeward for boats hidden behind the headsail.

Headsail trim

In most sail craft the headsail is the more important of the two in terms of drive. In order to obtain maximum drive, the sail must be set perfectly under each sailing condition and never more so than when working to windward, since it is the leading edge of this sail that determines how close to the wind the boat can point.

There are two factors which affect the sail shape — the halyard tension and the sheeting position. Since the halyard tension varies according to wind strength, this is dealt with separately. The sheeting position, generally speaking, remains the same through varying degrees of wind strengths and is only changed when the headsail is changed. As a general guide, there should be equal tension along the foot and the leech.

This cannot be determined correctly when rigging the boat so it will be necessary to make adjustments to the sheeting position during the tune-up period prior to the race. Moving the sheeting block forward along the track

Headsail trim is probably the most important single factor when working to windward. These J24s all have well set headsails which probably accounts for the closeness of the competition.

reduces the tension on the foot and increases the tension on the leech and vice versa. Some adjustment from this basic position may be necessary to keep the sail from binding on the spreader and thus losing its shape. On an average small keel boat, it is preferable to keep a gap of about 10 to 15 cm between the end of the spreader and the sail cloth, although this, like all factors concerning sail trim, may vary according to the type of boat and the size of the headsail in use.

Outside of this sheeting adjustment, the principal control of the headsail is achieved by the halyard or, if fitted, a Cunningham Eye purchase. The luff tension is varied according to the wind strength as follows:

Light Airs The luff tension must be eased to induce good shape into the sail, but not sufficiently to create wrinkles. Depending on the cut of the headsail, it may be wise to ease the sheet back a fraction to gain better shape and thus better drive, even at the risk of reducing pointing ability, for no matter how well the boat points if she does not move forward she will not be giving her best performance. It is far better to fall off a degree or two, fill the sail correctly and move along faster than to have her pointing high but with the wind skidding off the flattened sail and producing no drive.

Medium breezes As the wind increases in strength so the tension on the halyard or Cunningham purchase is increased. Likewise, the sail should be sheeted on harder so that the rough guide mentioned earlier — with the cloth of the sail just clear of the spreader — is retained.

Heavy winds These call for maximum tension on the halyard and/or Cunningham gear to obtain a 'knife edge' luff. The sheets should now be as tight as possible, without losing sight of the spreader/headsail relationship described earlier. As the wind increases it may be necessary to move the sheeting block aft a notch to 'bleed off' excessive wind at the top of the leech.

Mainsail trim

The indication of correct sail setting on the mainsail is best seen by the tufts. While large headsails may disturb the leeward tufts, particularly in the vicinity of the luff, the flow of wind over the mainsail will still show up on the remaining tufts.

As with the headsail, halyard and Cunningham purchase are used to adjust the luff tension on the mainsail. However, foot tension is controlled in this case by the clew outhaul, and the leech tension and shape by the main sheet and vang. Leech lines may be used to control leech flap but are rarely employed for changing the shape of the mainsail. Under differing wind conditions the setting of the mainsail should be along the following lines:

Light airs Ease the Cunningham purchase to the point where the luff is as slack as possible without wrinkling. The clew outhaul should be eased so that the foot of the mainsail is slackened to much the same degree. The traveller should be set either on the centre line or a little to windward providing the boom itself is not to windward of the centre line. A good guide is to set the second top batten in the fore and aft line of the boat, from which point adjustment of the sail will need only little sheet and vang tension.

Medium breezes As with the headsail, the increasing strength of wind requires increasing tension on the

Tufts are a good indication of mainsail trim although they can be disturbed by the backwind from large headsails.

Classic sail setting for medium weight breezes. Note how smoothly the slot between the sails funnels the air flow. Mainsheet traveller is about amidships, the boom vang or kicking strap just taking the weight.

Cunningham purchase with increased tension also on the clew outhaul. The traveller should be dropped a little to leeward and the boom vang tensioned to the same degree as the main sheet, so that if the sheet is eased the boom does not rise but runs out level.

Heavy winds In these conditions eveything must be under maximum tension. The traveller should be farther down to leeward and the vang tensioned so that it takes the weight as soon as the sheet is eased. Your biggest problem as skipper will be to overcome the tendency to 'kill' the boat by over-tension of the sheet. The ideal setting is something that will come only with experience, but having determined this setting it is a good idea to mark the sheet so that you have a reference point for future adjustment.

It goes without saying that the sheet must be used to reduce excessive heel by spilling wind when the counter-balancing effect of the crew weight is insufficient. Always bear in mind that the boat should be sailed as

Cats and centreboarders need to ease the mainsheet more than keelers to retain moderate heel. In most catamaran designs the mainsail, being the only sail, is the power unit and must be set and trimmed precisely for good performance.

upright as possible under the conditions. A boat that is lying on her ear flogging to windward may feel as though she is moving fast, but in fact is probably moving slower than she would if the main sheet were eased and the boat allowed to come more upright even if, temporarily, the main is flogging.

The psychological effect of being heeled hard over with spray flying everywhere and water rushing past along the lee gunwale is a false one in terms of forward speed. While the boat may be moving fast, the reduced lateral resistance on the keel is causing her to slip sideways through the water with the result that although she may be pointing high her course made good will be far lower than that of a boat which spills wind and remains closer to her optimum angle of heel.

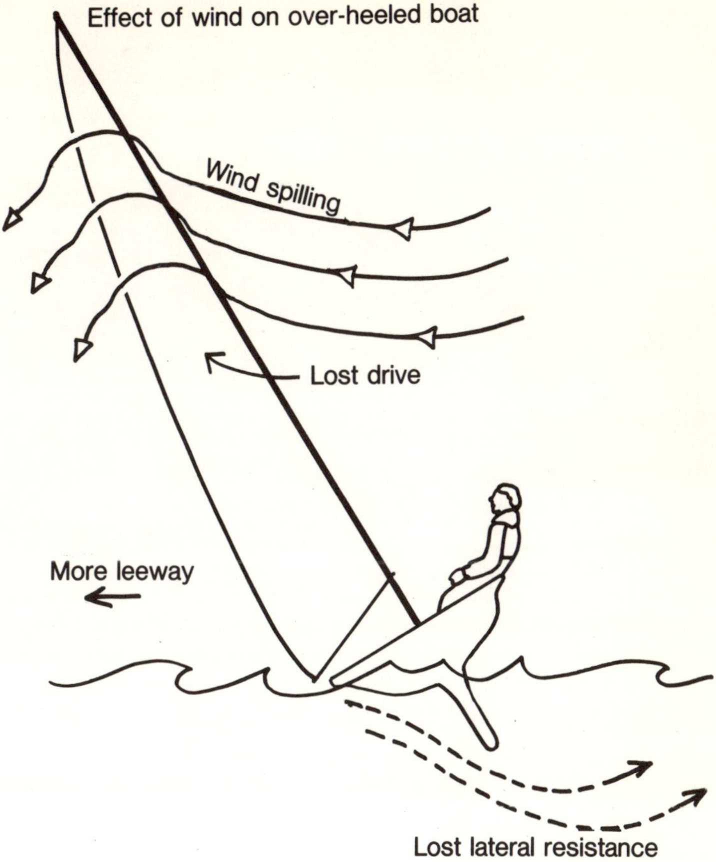

Heeling too far reduces the effective performance of the boat by reducing the lateral effect of the keel and spilling wind over the sail.

Backstay tension

The use of the backstay is important to sail trim in two principal ways. Increased tension on the backstay induces tension in the forestay and thus reduces luff sag with resultant improvement in pointing ability. It also promotes bend in the mast, particularly in fractional rigs, thus improving the performance of the sails under differing wind conditions.

The degree of mast bend varies from rig to rig and also according to wind strengths. Both sails are affected in a similar way — the greater the mast bend, the flatter the sail, which in turn moves the drive back from the luff. For this reason, backstay tension follows to a certain degree the

Speed is the important factor in light weather, pointing ability in medium breezes. Note different techniques in use here — leeward boat has slacked her Cunningham Eye and eased luff tension, has greater mast bend and two of three crew are up to windward.

formula for tensioning halyards or Cunningham purchases — in light weather only a little backstay tension is applied, the tension being increased more and more as the wind strength increases. Until you become familiar with the response of your own boat to backstay adjustment, a good practice is to watch other craft and learn to what degree the mast bend is used under differing conditions.

Basic techniques

There is a philosophy about windward work that is bandied around in yacht clubs and which offers excellent guide lines to novice racing skippers:

in light weather the aim is to go fast;
in medium weather the aim is to point high;
in heavy weather the aim is to avoid leeway.

In light weather you can afford to sail further in order to go faster. This means that if you can pick up speed by falling away from the wind, you should do so. Never sail too high

Wave slop has a particularly bad effect on small boats which lack the forward inertia of heavy keel boats. Riding a steep chop to minimise the effect is part of the skill of a racing helmsman.

or worry too much about pointing but concentrate always on improving your speed. A small increase in speed is much more significant in light weather than an extra degree of pointing ability.

In medium weather aim to get up to windward. Since most boats in these conditions are moving well, the advantage of falling away for an extra half-knot is lost. Concentrate now on pointing, by watching your sail tufts, watching the approaching weather and taking into consideration everything that might assist in getting higher to windward.

In heavy weather reduce the sail area and use your crew weight to keep the boat as upright as possible. Heeling too much causes the boat to slip sideways and is the greatest problem in gusty strong winds. Ease the main sheet where necessary and try to anticipate the gusts so that you ease before the gust strikes, thus preventing a sudden knock-down with the loss of optimum angle of heel. Using the mainsheet to keep the boat as upright as possible yet at the same time maintaining maximum drive is one of the secrets of sailing through gusty, strong winds.

Waves can also impede the boat's progress quite considerably. As a steep chop builds up the waves tend to batter against the bow, checking the boat's progress, particularly on a windward work. The longer waves of a swell cause the boat to slide down into the trough, stick her bow into the oncoming sea and shudder to a halt. A skilful helmsman will watch the waves approach closely and take action to avoid pounding or digging the boat's bow into the face of the wave. A good general technique is to luff slightly going up the face of a wave so that the detrimental effect of the oncoming wave is minimized, then fall away once over the crest to combine the added speed of the 'downhill' run and the increased drive from the wind.

Tacking

The most important single feature in racing to windward is tacking. In order to keep the boat moving she must always have a clear wind and in a crowded race, particularly after a windward start, this may mean tacking and tacking again to keep her clear of any congestion and foul wind from other boats. If tacking is done smoothly, it can gain tactical advantages as well as keeping the boat in a clear wind. The emphasis is, of course, on good technique. A bad tack can cost you time and position in a race, whereas a good tack may gain you as much as a length over a competitor.

You must not, of course, tack unnecessarily. There is no doubt that a boat which tacks will lose time to one that does not. However, assuming that all boats must make the same number of tacks then the important thing is to tack better than your competitors, in which case you gain time. Warn your crew well in advance, so that they have time to prepare and are keyed up for the tacking manoeuvre. Ensure that all gear is free to run smoothly and that there will be no knots in sheets or similar problems which can hold the boat in the middle of the manoeuvre and bring her to a dead stop.

The first basic maxim of good tacking is to sail the boat round using an easy sweeping manoeuvre on the helm rather than a sudden thrust to leeward. The flow of water over the rudder must not be disturbed more than necessary, for any turbulence acts as a brake and will slow the boat in the turn. The helm should be put down easily and the boat brought up smoothly to the wind, sweeping round in a tight but easy circle. As soon as the bow starts to run up, the leeward sheet is released and the opposite sheet pulled on, although if it is pulled on too early it will back the headsail and bring the boat to a dead stop.

There are many expert skippers who will disagree with releasing the sheet so soon. Some prefer to hold the leeward sheet until the sail is almost backed. Much depends, of course, on the size and type of boat and the size of headsail. However, keeping the headsail on after the boat has started her turn to windward is only utilizing sideways wind caused by the boat's turn which has no drive and may even have a slightly detrimental effect.

In light airs it may be necessary to hold the headsail until backed in order to push the bow through the wind, but under normal circumstances the boat should have sufficient way to carry her round easily without the need for any attempt to obtain further drive from the headsail.

When the boat comes through her tack, she will be almost stopped and will need to fall off slightly to get moving again. Easing the main slightly will give her a quick pickup; sheeting on the jib will add to this and start her moving almost immediately. Avoid sheeting any sails too hard, for at this stage sheets that are slightly 'sprung' will give the sail a fullness that will gather up wind and get her moving while a flattened sail will only cause the wind to skid off, producing little drive. As soon as the boat gathers speed, the sheets must be trimmed and the boat returned to her optimum sailing position.

Rounding the mark

Probably the most important psychological factor in approaching a mark is to maintain your concentration. There are lots of distractions at this point in the race — boats closing from all directions, overlaps and other rules being claimed and probably on your own boat last-minute preparations for setting the spinnaker. Such distractions must be kept in proportion or your concentration, and that of your crew, will lapse and the boat will lose speed and position. At this critical point there will probably be boats pressing hard on your tail, even as you are pressing hard on the boat in front. A moment's distraction, a slight deviation from course or slowing down in speed, and you

Two J24s illustrate the rights and wrongs of tacking:
(a) Boat 336 prepared to tack, 298 will cover him. Note how one skipper sits to windward, one to leeward.

(b) 298 sweeps round faster than 336. He also has a man forward helping the headsail round, 336 has a man doing nothing!

(c) 298 is almost round and sheeting on, 336 is still turning.

(d) 298 has his headsail drawing and will pull away from 336 who is still turning and has not sheeted on properly as yet.

Close tacking is a part of windward work and calls for good timing and steady nerves.

have dropped back one position in the race! By the same token, maintaining close concentration and keeping the boat moving fast gives you the opportunity of gaining a place if there is a lapse on the part of one of the skippers ahead of you.

The windward mark may be rounded either on the port or starboard hand and different techniques are required for each. With a port hand rounding (leaving the mark to port), the fleet will close and form a starboard tack 'queue' on the approach to the buoy. If your approach is on a starboard tack, then you simply join the 'queue' and battle your way round as best you can. If your last leg is a port tack, there are two options open. In the first you simply watch your opportunity to tack and join the 'queue' which is probably the safest approach, particularly if there are sizable gaps between the other boats. The second option is to approach the buoy on a port tack and make a close tack around the buoy, squeezing yourself in at the last moment.

This is a somewhat risky business since the other boats will be laying the buoy and leave you little room to get in unless a fortuitous gap appears at the right moment. One advantage that can be gained, however, is by making your final tack outside two boat lengths of the mark in which case you can claim 'buoy room' on any closing yachts.

There is less likely to be a 'queue' of boats when rounding a starboard hand mark since there are definite advantages to be gained by approaching on a starboard tack while the queue must form on port tack. If you do approach on port tack, watch for a starboard tack boat coming up on the inside approach and forcing you to give way. Undoubtedly the best approach to this mark is on a starboard tack as you have right of way.

When rounding either mark it is important to remember that too severe a helm action reduces the efficiency of the rudder and acts as a brake. A smooth helm operation which turns the boat cleanly and steadily rather than jerking her around savagely keeps her moving fast with a good water flow across the rudder surface. Trimming the sheets at the same time and in much the same manner keeps the power flowing and the boat speed at a maximum. Sheets which are eased too rapidly will luff and lose efficiency, while sheets that are not eased fast enough will produce a braking effect since they are not set to derive full power from the wind. It is most important to remember at this stage that your crew's efficiency on the sheets will have as much effect on the boat's performance as your helm actions. So if a spinnaker is to be set, ensure that the work is properly delegated and you do not have all hands racing forward to set the 'kite', leaving the jib and mainsheets to their own devices.

5 Basic Tactics

Almost all basic racing tactics can be summed up in two philosophies:

1 Sail the shortest possible course.

2 Keep the boat in clear wind.

Paradoxically, these should really come in the reverse order, with priority placed on keeping the boat in a clear wind. You would not sail in the wind shadow of another boat simply to retain the best course, but tack into clear wind even at the expense of taking a less desirable course. However, the basic tactics of a windward work are probably best explained by dealing first with tactics aimed at reaching the buoy in the shortest possible time assuming you have a completely free run.

Sailing the best course

Since it is impossible to sail straight to the windward mark, your aim must always be to steer the most desirable course — the one which takes you closest to the mark. The most favourable tack is the one which has the boat's bow pointing closest to the mark and the time to tack is when this favourable tack reaches the point when the boat points closer to the mark on the opposite tack. The secret, obviously, is to know how well your boat points so that you can determine the exact time to change tack. The point at which the boat can be tacked to lay the mark exactly will vary according to her distance away. In diagrammatic form, the 'lay lines' form the sides of a triangle radiating outwards from the windward mark beyond which you should never sail. The windward work should remain entirely within these two lines.

Wind shifts are generally described as 'lifts' if they enable you to point higher towards the mark and 'knocks' or 'headers' if they make it necessary to fall away. Obviously, a lift is always beneficial, while a knock will place you in a dilemma as to whether your adjusted course is still the most favourable or whether you should tack, hoping that the shift is not just a temporary one. Being

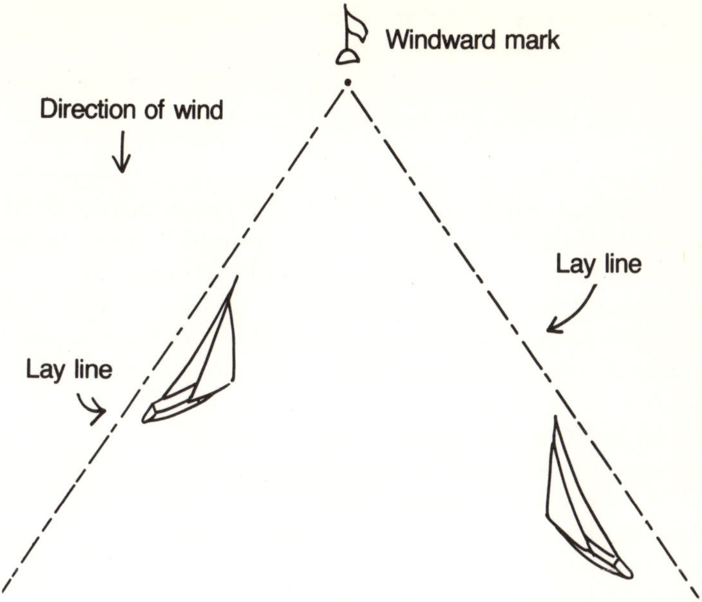

Illustrating the lay lines within which a windward work should be made.

knocked or 'headed' often creates considerable tactical problems, for apart from altering what was a favourable heading, it has also altered the relationship of other boats to your own. A quick reassessment of the whole situation, and in particular knowing precisely how your boat will point on the new course, will indicate whether to stay on the current course or make a quick tack.

Tides and tidal flow

Tidal problems and the way in which they affect your windward work are mostly more predictable. While there is always the risk of tidal eddies or anomalies, particularly in rivers and estuaries, these are usually temporary and in the main tidal movements are fairly predictable. By and large water runs faster in deep channels than in the shallow areas and for the most part sweeps wide around bends.

The traditional Rule of Twelfths which predicts that the change in the height of tides between successive low and high waters is in the proportion of one-twelfth in the first hour, two-twelfths in the second hour, three in the third and fourth hours, two in the fifth and one in the sixth hour (1–2–3–3–2–1) indicates that the speed of the tidal flow will be faster in the third and fourth hours of change and less towards the slack waters of high and low tides. From this, and using local tidal predictions (the emphasis is on *local*, since tidal predictions can vary greatly between waterways only a mile or two apart) you should be able to determine what effect the tide will have on your course.

Obviously, local knowledge is a vital factor where tidal flow is concerned. This can only be gained by experience or by studying local conditions and obtaining local assistance. If you bear in mind the Rule of Twelfths, the faster flow of spring tides as opposed to neaps, and the fact that rivers will probably have a faster ebb flow than flood, particularly after heavy rain fall, you will have covered most of the basics. So many factors are involved, however, that it would be easy to write a book on the tidal flow of almost every estuary and river; so local knowledge is the key if you are racing in unfamiliar waters.

Common sense will dictate your tactics once you have determined what effect the tide will have on you at different points along the course. Obviously these effects

Local knowledge can play a big part in winning a race. Sailing hard up under a high cliff, for example, may provide a totally dead lee or bad knocks, but on the other hand can provide race-winning lifts. Tidal flows can produce similar confusing effects.

are not confined solely to the windward leg, but are common along the length of the course and will similarly require an assessment of their effect on each different leg.

Keeping a clear wind

The most important factor in any aspect of racing, and the one which has the greatest importance particularly on the windward leg, is keeping the boat in clear wind. If you find yourself in an opponent's wind shadow, or any other situation where the boat cannot sail at her best, then break tack and sail away into clear wind even if it involves tacking on to a less favourable course.

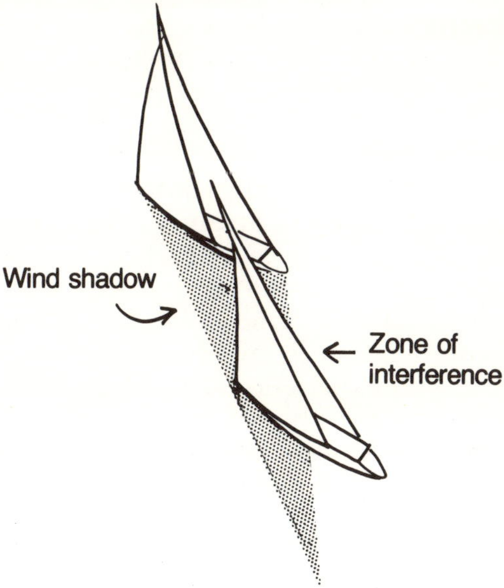

Wind shadow from a sail has a surprisingly limited effect on nearby boats.

By the same token, it is good tactics to try and foul-wind an opponent and force him to tack on to a less favoured course. But never go out of your way to achieve such a result, for more races are lost by boats becoming involved in 'personal' duels than those that keep their sights firmly on the best course to the windward mark. In the excitement and exhilaration of a duel it is easy to get carried away from your prime objective and forget, until they are way ahead of you, that there are other boats in the race.

If things get too hectic and you cannot get a clear wind, then you are better to break away into open space rather than battle through congested space and turbulent air.

Tack and counter tack

Experience pays off tremendously in tactical racing. A typical example is involved in giving way to a crossing starboard tack. You can bear away early to pass under his stern rather than leave it to the last moment when you will be forced to tack and almost inevitably find yourself in his wind shadow, putting him in an advantageous position. By the same token, with experience and judgement, you can close up to him, tack quickly and put yourself into the safe leeward position and lee-bow him thus giving yourself the advantage. It goes without saying that a fine degree of

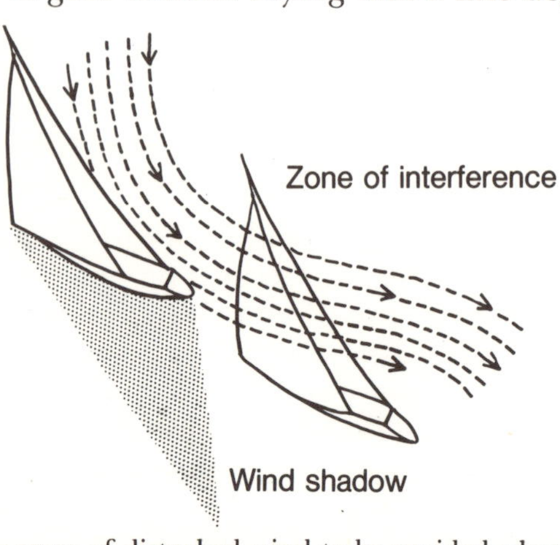

Indicating the areas of disturbed wind to be avoided when attempting to overtake.

judgement is required to perfect such manoeuvres, but this is the stuff that tactical sailboat racing is made of.

A similar situation can arise when you are being overtaken by an obviously faster boat. You have the right to luff him until his helmsman is abeam of your mast — 'mast abeam' — but at this point you fall into his wind shadow and lose a considerable amount of time. If it is inevitable that he is going to pass you, it is better to anticipate the situation and tack away into a clear wind before he bears down on you. Even if he is an opponent in your race, the luffing match will only forestall an inevitable break by one or the other, and in the meantime lose speed for both. As mentioned, private duels between two boats often result in both being disadvantaged to the benefit of the rest of the fleet.

Much the same applies to the tactic of getting away from the rest of the fleet. It is a basic maxim to keep as close as you can to your most respected opponents and even if you are behind, you will rarely benefit by shooting off on your own. While you may sail way out and be lucky enough to pick up a chance advantageous wind shift, the odds are against it. Far more can be gained by keeping close to your opponents, watching their every move and taking advantage of any opportunities that may crop up during close manoeuvring.

'Covering' your opponent can, when properly practised, keep him in a disadvantaged position or cause him to lose speed and distance in breaking away from your cover. If you are being covered yourself, try a few 'sneaky' — but quite legitimate — tactics such as making a false tack. Have your crew ready at the tacking positions, make a great show of preparing to tack, even put the helm down briefly to create a luff, then immediately swing back on course! If the covering boat falls for your dummy and goes into a tack you will leave behind an infuriated but well-beaten opponent!

As with all aspects of racing, it would be easy to write a whole book on tactics and indeed, the novice racing skipper should study all available works on the subject. But without doubt, common sense and basic sailing principles, many of which are taken for granted and therefore not mentioned in books on advanced racing techniques, count for much. For example, a skipper who blindly stares at his

To tack or not to tack is quite definitely the question here. Boat 1842 has the option of bearing away to pass under 1687 or tacking quickly in the hope of lee-bowing him.

tufts throughout the whole race and never takes time out to watch what is going on around him will sail a good course but will be pushed all over the place by smarter tacticians.

Apart from watching the movements of your opponents, keep an eye out for boats way up ahead in another race. These will indicate the likely winds you will encounter as you move in that direction and enable you to anticipate shifts and be prepared for them before the skipper who looks no farther than his forestay. There is so much for the racing skipper to do that he may well wonder if he has the physical attributes to cope with it all. With practice, however, many reactions become instinctive and the initial concentration and effort become second nature. Someone once said if an octopus had eight eyes he would make an ideal racing helmsman. That, perhaps, adequately sums up the situation.

6 Off The Wind

As the boat falls off the wind and the spinnaker is set, the headsail should be dropped as soon as possible. While some skippers carry the headsail inside the spinnaker, particularly on a close reach, this is not advisable since the spinnaker relies on a smooth flow of air and any sail on the forestay is liable to disturb this flow. When handed, the headsail must be secured or it may slip overboard and trail in the water, unseen by a crew intent on watching the luff of the spinnaker. Similarly, headsail sheets must be brought inboard, for an 'Irish Pennant' can make a difference between two boats which are otherwise performing identically.

Carrying a headsail inside the spinnaker rarely works successfully. The spinnaker, being a light-weight, full-cut sail, requires a totally undisturbed air flow to set properly.

A secondary spinnaker, usually called a 'blooper' or 'big boy', will not disturb the airflow in the main spinnaker and can frequently be carried on a downwind run adding to the boat's performance.

Trimming the spinnaker

The basic setting of the spinnaker is with the tack and clew at the same height and with the pole set so that a line between the tack and the clew is at right angles to the apparent wind. For most purposes the pole should be set level, although in certain light weather conditions an advantage can be gained by raising the outboard end of the pole.

On the off-wind legs, the spinnaker is the most important sail on the boat, and must be kept drawing to its maximum as is the headsail when working to windward. As with all sails, maximum drive from the spinnaker lies close to the luff and once the sail has been set up, the sheet must be eased gradually until the luff begins to collapse. A

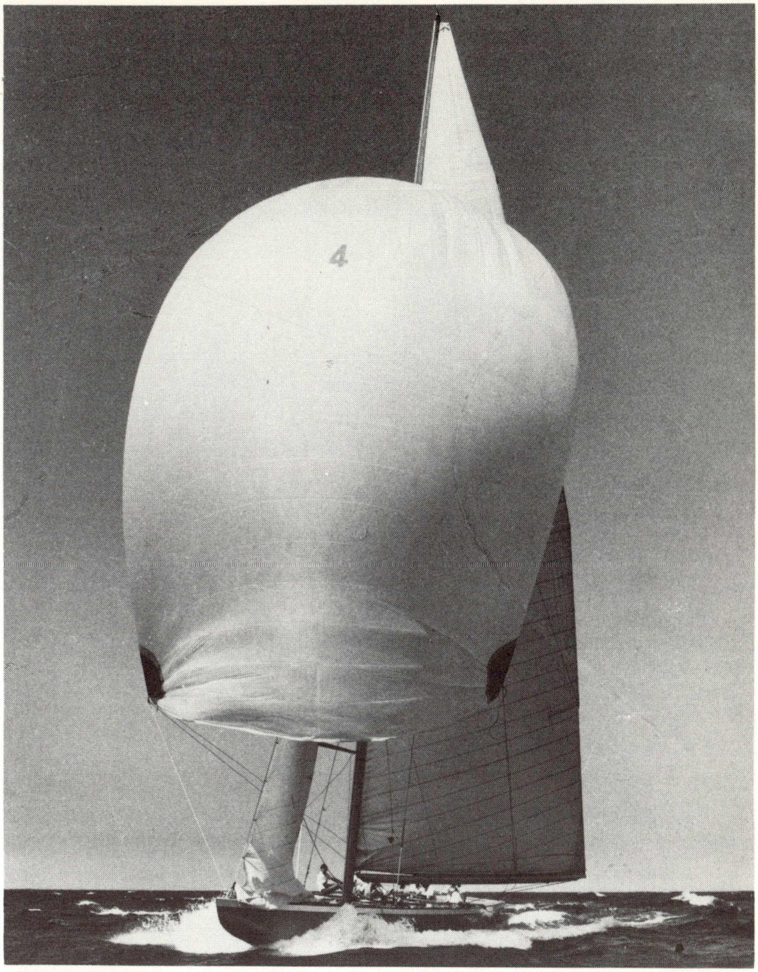

Illustrating the enormous power of a spinnaker drawing to capacity, a 12 metre gets up on the plane and literally flies across the water.

short, sharp jerk is probably all that is needed to refill the sail at which point the sheet is eased again and the procedure repeated. Anticipation is the key to efficient spinnaker flying, for if the sail folds and collapses you will need to take in so much sheet to recover it that when it refills it will be sheeted far too tightly and efficiency will be lost. By watching the luff closely and moving swiftly as it begins to collapse, such a happening can be avoided.

Of course, a sudden wind shift may cause the spinnaker to collapse, in which case sheet adjustment will not be

Carrying a big spinnaker 'shy' — on a broad reach — creates enormous stresses on the rig. Gear must be in perfect condition and crew trained well in spinnaker handling or disastrous situations can develop under these conditions.

sufficient to refill it. The pole will need to be adjusted, or if the sail cannot be 'shied' any more, the boat must fall off. Wind shifts are as much a feature of the off-wind leg as they are of the windward leg and adjustments to the pole may be necessary on a number of occasions if the sail is to be kept drawing to its maximum at all times.

Trimming the mainsail

Although the spinnaker is the most important sail, the main must also receive close attention for it has an important part to play. The Cunningham Eye should be eased and the traveller moved down to leeward while the vang tension should be taken up but with no pressure applied. The mainsheet should be eased as far as possible to keep the tufts streaming evenly on either side of the sail — but avoiding one of the most common mistakes beginners to racing make when they keep the mainsail sheeted too hard.

When the boat is running dead square downwind, the pole and the main boom must be squared out on either side. The vang again is tensioned but not pressured and the crew move aft to counteract the tendency of the wind to push the bow down. One of the major problems on a square run is the tendency of the boat to roll; this can be minimized by keeping the crew weight into the centre of the boat and as low as possible. To avoid oscillation of the spinnaker head, which in turn can set up a rolling syndrome, the tweakers should be pulled hard down to tension the outside edges of the sail.

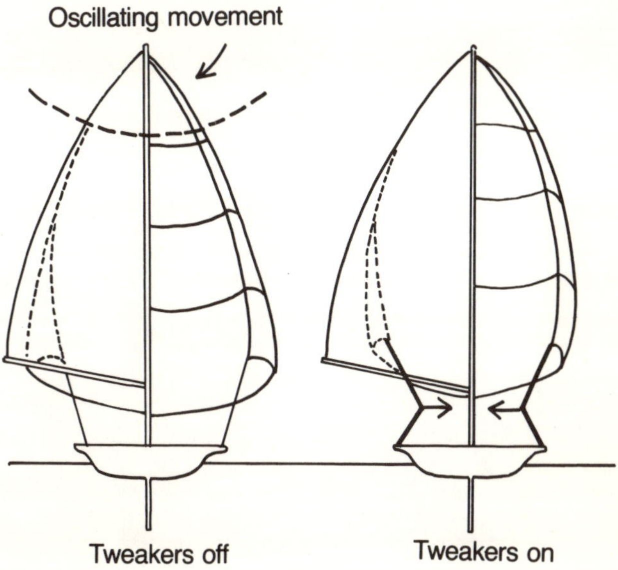

Tweakers tension the brace or guy as well as the sheet and thus reduce the tendency for oscillation at the head of the spinnaker.

Another problem is the possibility of running 'by the lee'. Apart from being a dangerous situation, this reduces the efficiency of the boat and gybing — even at the risk of having to do so twice or more on the leg — is preferable. The disadvantages of running 'by the lee' or even dead square downwind are indicated by the fact that many skippers prefer, in light airs, to sail with the wind on the quarter and induce an extra gybe, for the extra distance involved is more than compensated for by the additional speed gained.

Tactics

Since a straight line is the shortest between two points, the direct line between two marks on the off-wind leg is the one to follow. There is a tendency even among experienced skippers to edge to windward, because the leading boats will be caught in the wind shadow of those following. Try not to be involved in this trend, for apart from sailing a longer course than necessary, edging to windward means that the last lap must be made virtually on a square run — the slowest point of sailing for any boat. If it is necessary to digress from the line at all, it is

Radial head spinnakers are currently the most popular.

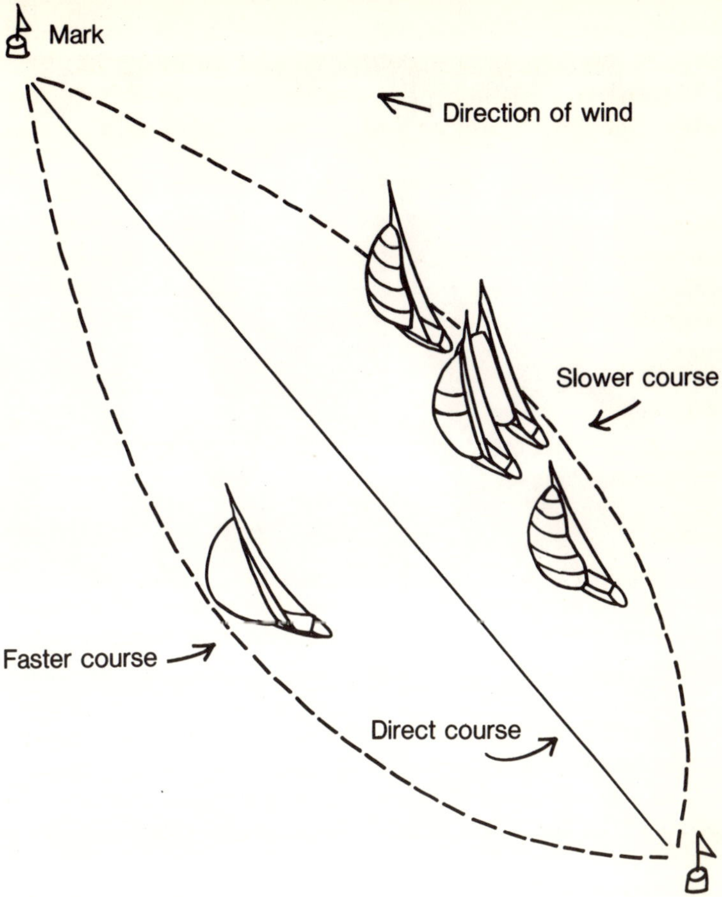

Worrying about the wind shadow of following boats, many race leaders tend to edge to windward on the downwind run. This leaves the leeward area clear which, paradoxically, is the better area in which to sail.

far better to edge away to leeward, for here there are two distinct advantages to be gained: on the approach to the buoy you will be tightening the sheets and thus moving faster,. and you will also be lying on the inside berth. While it is important to keep a clear wind, the effect of the wind shadow from another yacht's sails is often over estimated. As a general rule, the cone of a wind shadow is usually only about three mast heights, reducing, of course, with the taper of the cone. An obvious tactical manoeuvre is to try and throw your wind shadow on the boat in front, thus collapsing his spinnaker and enabling you to race past. However, rest assured that no sooner are you ahead than

The cone or wind shadow is often far less than anticipated as illustrated by these three boats, all of which would appear to be sailing in foul air — a fact discredited by their full 'kites'.

he will refill his spinnaker and repay you the compliment! This dog-eat-dog manoeuvring gains little on the main part of the off-wind leg and is best practised on the approach to the mark when the boat you overtake has no time to turn the tables.

In strong wind gusts a considerable advantage can be gained by pulling away — this lessens the pressure on the boat which causes her to heel or risk a broach. This tactic will also enable her to stay in the strong gust longer; then as the wind eases, to pull up and sheet on again. If a squall causes her to broach, the mainsheet must be eased quickly to avoid rounding up and total collapse of the spinnaker.

Rounding the mark

Rounding a leeward mark differs from rounding a windward mark principally in the approach. Where on the windward mark you have no choice but to approach as closely as possible, on the leeward mark it is wise where possible to approach wide and harden up on the mark as you turn. This, of course, will depend greatly on other boats around you but if the turn can be achieved smoothly and with good trimming of the sheets a definite advantage

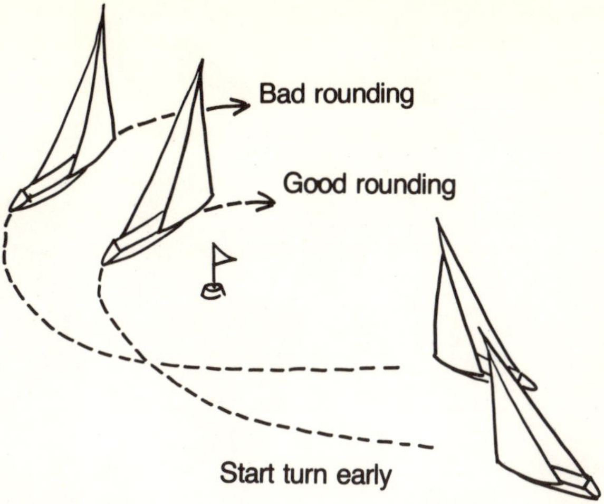

Sweep wide on the approach to the downwind mark, tightening up as you turn and leaving no gap between you and the buoy for following boats to squeeze through.

and possibly an inside berth can be gained. The question of when to drop the spinnaker is dependent purely on the expertise of your crew, for it is necessary to have the sail handed and secured and the headsail up and trimmed correctly before rounding the mark or you will lose speed and efficiency at a time which can cause serious problems. The time lost by dropping the spinnaker early will be regained if your crew are in position and trimming the headsail and mainsail sheets smoothly as you turn around the mark, although obviously the longer you can hang on to the spinnaker while achieving this end result, the better. The answer lies in efficient crew training and practice.

While approaching the mark wide and hardening up to close with it on the turn is preferable, it may not always be possible. Rounding close on the mark means that you sweep wide on the far side thus allowing following boats to take the inside berth. Turning hard around the buoy, on the proverbial sixpence, is no solution to that problem, for such a hard turn inevitably tends almost to stop the boat dead. The fierce action of the helm creates a braking effect on the rudder, while the crew cannot sheet on hard enough and fast enough to keep the boat moving

The mark is just ahead and spinnakers are about to be handed. Hanging on too long before dousing the kite can cause enormous problems at the mark. Better to have it down and stowed with headsail sheeted so you can cut through those boats that are still struggling to hand the big sail.

smoothly. Always the secret is to keep the boat moving fast and easily, even if in so doing you allow room for other boats to move through. In cases like this it becomes a question of which is the lesser of two evils and by keeping the boat moving at least you stay up with the fleet, even if conceding a slight advantage; whereas by stopping the boat in a hard turn the rest of the fleet will leave you wallowing. Always, under any difficult condition — not necessarily even rounding a mark — one of the major secrets of successful racing is to keep the boat moving fast.

7 Loose Ends

Finishing

Rather like the starting line, the finishing line will almost certainly have one end more favourable than another. Obviously the most advantageous end is the one you can get to quickest — in other words, the end closest to you as you race along the final leg of the course. Since you will not be in a position to determine beforehand which end is more favourable — as is the case prior to starting — it will be a question of judgement, and weighing prevailing conditions in order to determine which end of the line to aim for.

The final leg is the one, more than any other, where you must utilise every tactic to keep your nose in front of other boats. Where earlier there may have been little point in

The race for the line. With clear wind it is simply a question of getting the maximum out of the boat. With the competition breathing down your neck you may need to pull every tactical trick in the book.

engaging in a tough 'luffing match' with an overtaking boat, now, if such a tactic holds him off until you get your nose across the line then it is a worthwhile exercise. Similarly in a tacking duel it may be worth covering a close competitor in order to hold him in a disadvantaged position for the few hundred metres it takes to reach the line. However, private 'duels' rarely pay off even at this stage for the only boats to win when you go out on a limb to beat a close competitor are those that slip by while you are engaged in your duel.

Where a large number of boats are heading to the line together you may have to work your tactics on a 'percentage' basis. For example, it is better to let one boat through in order to beat the others rather than beating one and allowing three to go through. As with starting, a starboard tack always has the advantage over port tack when the final approach is a windward work.

Above and opposite: Blanketing an opponent only works if you are so close to the line that he cannot do the same to you.
(a) 2109 manoeuvres to blanket 2712.

(b) The manoeuvre pays off and 2712 loses his spinnaker.

(c) 2109 is through and flying, but now 2712 will attempt to turn the tables by blanketing 2109.

On a downwind run the blanketing of an opponent close ahead to 'kill' his spinnaker should be held off until the last moment so that he has no time to recover and return the compliment before you cross the line.

'Shooting' the line is a desperate measure that can gain a few winning centimetres in the last breath of the race. Rather like a runner leaning forward to touch the finishing tape with any part of his body and gain an extra centimetre or two over a rival who remains upright, shooting the finish involves throwing the boat head to wind when approaching the finishing line in a duel. Make sure, however, if you employ this technique that the boat has sufficient way to carry her across the line, for to fall short would be both frustrating and embarrassing. A similar tactic used at one end of the line when the buoy or finish boat necessitates another tack can add that all important advantage over a rival who makes the extra tack. In this case, however, make sure the boat does not fall down on the mark for the racing rules still apply at this stage.

Post-mortem

On the way back to the club house after the finish of a race, skipper and crew should get down to an immediate post-mortem to sort out the mistakes that were made and make sure that they are not made again. Leaving the post-mortem until later is never quite as satisfactory, for memories become dulled with time and club house beverage, whereas immediately after the finish everyone in the crew is analysing what happened regardless of whether you won or lost.

Another good wrinkle at this point is to jot down in a notebook any repair or maintenance work, or adjustment to the gear that should be done before the next race. Once again time and other interests tend to divert the mind from such necessary requirements and you will find yourself going out to the next race suddenly aware that the work has not been done. A winch that jams, a sheet that over-rides or a halyard that is showing signs of wear can be brought up as part of the post-mortem discussion and jotted down in a notebook to ensure that they are fixed before the start of the next race.

While the post-mortem by the crew of your own boat will perhaps be the most in-depth analysis of what went wrong (or otherwise!), inevitably a broader discussion and theoretical re-enactment of the race will take place with other boat crews in the club house. Such analytical discussions can be very useful to racing newcomers, and as such your ear should be keenly tuned to pick up snippets of useful information which will be thrown out by more experienced racing men.

The racing rules

Intelligent use of the racing rules is a large part of racing tactics. While the rules are not made to be broken, they can be used to the utmost limit to gain an advantage over a close competitor. It follows, then, that you should be totally conversant with every one of the rules and their application when an occasion to use them arises. Since such an occasion will almost invariably be in the heat of the fray, only a skipper with a cool head and a complete familiarity with the rule book will be able to utilise the rules to his advantage.

Applying the rules in the course of a race varies considerably according to the conditions at the time, the

Knowing the racing rules thoroughly and putting them into practice to gain advantage in the heat of a race is a major tactic in racing. Here boat 159 has tacked in the middle of a leg for some tactical reason — perhaps to 'wrong foot' the following boats on port tack, or gain a clear wind or work a tide. . . .

proximity and approach of other boats and the particular leg of the course which is being sailed, or mark which is being rounded. While there may be certain 'set' pieces or movements which can be used to gain a tactical advantage, in most cases a decision on the use of a rule or rules to disadvantage a competitor must be judged by the skipper on the spur of the moment. There are numerous excellent books on racing tactics and the use of the rules and these will be necessary reading if you plan to improve your racing ability. However, as a beginner — and that is what this book is all about — the only book you should read and absorb thoroughly is the rule book itself! Without a total knowledge of every rule applicable to the course along which you are racing and the ability to identify a situation where the use of a rule can gain an advantage, you will not improve your racing tactics beyond your sailing ability and the speed of your boat. Since, as mentioned, use of the rules is a vitally important part of racing tactics, until you have achieved this familiarity in using the rules you will place yourself at a disadvantage against skippers with more experience.